Selected Poems

Selected Poems

Paul Auster

faber and faber

This edition first published in 1998
by Faber and Faber Limited
3 Queen Square London WC1N 3AU

These poems were published in 1990 in *Ground Work:
Selected Poems and Essays 1970–1979*

The selection of poems reproduces the contents of
Disappearances: Selected Poems 1970–1979
(Overlook, 1988), which was in turn culled from
the following books, previously published in the USA:
Unearth (Living Hand, 1974); *Wall Writing* (The
Figures, 1976); *Fragments from Cold* (Parenthèse, 1977);
White Spaces (Station Hill, 1980); *Facing the Music* (Station
Hill, 1980); 'Spokes' originally appeared in *Poetry*.

Photoset by Wilmaset Ltd, Wirral
Printed in Great Britain by
Mackays of Chatham PLC Chatham, Kent

A CIP record for this book
is available from the British Library

ISBN 0-571-19509-1

10 9 8 7 6 5 4 3 2 1

Contents

Poems

Poems

Spokes

Roots writhe with the worm – the sift
Of the clock cohabits the sparrow's heart.
Between branch and spire – the word
Belittles its nest, and the seed, rocked
By simpler confines, will not confess.
Only the egg gravitates.

*

In water – my absence in aridity. A flower.
A flower that defines the air.
In the deepest well, your body is fuse.

*

The bark is not enough. It furls
Redundant shards, will barter
Rock for sap, blood for veering sluice,
While the leaf is pecked, brindled
With air, and how much more, furrowed
Or wrapped, between dog and wolf,
How much longer will it stake
The axe to its gloating advantage?

*

Nothing waters the bole, the stone wastes nothing.
Speech could not cobble the swamp,
And so you dance for a brighter silence.
Light severs wave, sinks, camouflages –
The wind clacks, is bolt.
I name you desert.

*

Picks jot the quarry – eroded marks
That could not cipher the message.
The quarrel unleashed its alphabet,
And the stones, girded by abuse,
Have memorized the defeat.

*

Drunk, whiteness hoards its strength,
When you sleep, sun drunk, like a seed
That holds its breath
Beneath the soil. To dream in heat
All heat
That infests the equilibrium
Of a hand, that germinates
The miracle of dryness...
In each place you have left
Wolves are maddened
By the leaves that will not speak.
To die. To welcome red wolves
Scratching at the gates: howling
Page – or you sleep, and the sun
Will never be finished.
It is green where black seeds breathe.

*

The flower is red, is perched
Where roots split, in the gnarl
Of a tower, sucking in its meager fast,
And retracting the spell
That welds step to word
And ties the tongue to its faults.
The flower will be red
When the first word tears the page,
Will thrive in the ooze, take color,
Of a lesioned beak, when the sparrow
Is bloodied, and flies from one
Earth into the bell.

*

Between the sparrow and the bird without name:
its prey.

Light escapes through the interval.

*

Each trance pales in the hub, the furtive
Equinox of names: pawl
Thwarting ratchet – jarring skies that orb
This austere commerce with wind.
Lulls mend. But gales nourish
Chance: breath, blooming, while the wheel scores
Its writing into earth. Bound back
To your feet. Eyes tend soil
In the cool of dying suns. The song
Is in the step.

*

Embering to the lip
Of nether sky – the undevoured nest-light
Ebbs to sustenance: from the sparrow
To the bird without name, the interval
Is prey – smoke
That softens coals, unlike the sect
Of wings, where you beat, smoke wed
To glow – in the sparrow's memory
It perfects the sleep of clouds.

*

To see is this other torture, atoned for
In the pain of being seen: the spoken,
The seen, contained in the refusal
To speak, and the seed of a single voice,
Buried in a random stone.
My lies have never belonged to me.

*

Into the hub the shell implodes,
Endures as a pun of loam and rock,
Rising as stick, to invade, to drive
Out the babble that worded its body
To emerge, to wait for future
Blows – city in root, in deed, unsprung, even out
Of the city. Get out. The wheel
Was deception. It cannot turn.

*

The egg limits renunciation, cannot
Sound in another's ringing, the least
Hammering, before the wail slits
Its course, and the eye squanders
The subterfuge of a longer lamp.
Lifted into speech, it carries
Its own birth, and if it shatters
Acclaim its fall and contradiction.
Your earth will always be far.

Unearth

1 Along with your ashes, the barely
   written ones, obliterating
   the ode, the incited roots, the alien
   eye – with imbecilic hands, they dragged you
   into the city, bound you in
   this knot of slang, and gave you
   nothing. Your ink has learned
   the violence of the wall. Banished,
   but always to the heart
   of brothering quiet, you cant the stones
   of unseen earth, and smooth your place
   among the wolves. Each syllable
   is the work of sabotage.

II Flails, the whiteness, the flowers
of the promised land: and all
you hoard, crumbling at the brink
of breath. For a single word
in air we have not breathed, for one
stone, splitting with the famine
inside us – ire,
out of bone's havoc, by which we kin
the worm. The wall
is your only witness. Barred
from me, but squandering nothing,
you sprawl over each unwritten page,
as though your voice had crawled
from you: and entered the whiteness
of the wail.

III Vatic lips, weaned
of image. The mute one
here, who waits, urn-wise,
in wonder. Curse overbrims
prediction: the glacial rose
bequeaths its thorns to the breath
that labors toward eye
and oblivion.
We have only to ready ourselves.
From the first step, our voice
is in league
with the stones of the field.

IV Night, as though tasted
within. And of us, each lie
the tongue would know
when it draws back, and sinks
into its poison.
We would sleep, side by side
with such hunger, and from the fruit
we war with, become the name
of what we name. As though a crime, dreamed
by us, could ripen in cold, and fell
these black, roweling trees
that drain the history of stars.

v Unquelled
   in this flood of earth –
   where seeds end
   and augur nearness – you will sound
   the choral rant
   of memory, and go the way
   that eyes go. There is no longer
   path for you: from the moment
   you slit your veins, roots will begin
   to recite the massacre
   of stones. You will live. You will build
   your house here – you will forget
   your name. Earth
   is the only exile.

VI Thistle, drenched by heat,
    and the barren word
    that prods you – shouted
    down to the lodes.
    Light would spill here.
    It would seep through
    the scrawled branch that wrote
    such cowering above us.
    As if, far from you,
    I could feel it breaking
    through me, as I walked
    north into my body.

VII Between these spasms
of light, in brittle fern, in dark
thickets: waiting
in your labyrinthine ear
for the thunder
to crack: for the Babel-roar,
for the silence. It will not
be what you wandered to
that is heard. But the step,
burrowing under
this parted sky, that keeps its distance
whole. And that widens in you
at the mouth
of cloven earth, where you watch
these fallen stars
struggle to crawl back to you,
bearing the gifts of hell.

VIII Ice – means nothing
   is miracle, if it must
   be what will – you are the means
   and the wound – opening
   out of ice, and the cadence through
   blunt earth, when crows
   come to maraud. Wherever you walk, green
   speaks into you, and holds. Silence
   stands the winter eye to eye
   with spring.

IX Scrolls of your second earth, unraveled
by my slow, incendiary hands.
The sky in your name – sliding down
scarps of blueness: the sky
overroaring wheat.
Do not ask – for what. Say nothing –
watch. Parades of the beaten,
for whom I tore apart
the drum. Your other life, glowing in the fuse
of this one. The unbaked loaves: the retina's lack
of solace.

x Wind-spewn, from the radiant
no, and grafted on
the brown-green scar of this
moment. You ask
what place this is, and I, along the seams
of your dismembering,
have told you: the forest
is the memory
of itself, this frail
splinter, streaming through
my navigable blood, and driven
aground in heart-rubble. You ask
words of me, and I
will speak them – from the moment
I have learned
to give you nothing.

XI From one stone touched
to the next stone
named: earth-hood: the inaccessible
ember. You
will sleep here, a voice
moored to stone, moving through
this empty house that listens
to the fire that destroyed it. You
will begin. To drag your body
from the ashes. To carry the burden
of eyes.

XII Prayer-grown –
   in the ghost-written tract
   of your somewhere,
   in the landscape
   where you will not stand – whorl-bits
   of ammonite
   reinvent you.
   They roll you along
   with earth's mock caroling
   underfoot, scattering
   the hundred-faced lie
   that makes you visible. And from each
   daylight blow, your hardness turns
   to weapon, another slum
   flowers within. (Prayer-grown –
   the clandestine word, as though cutting
   through the hand
   that groped along these cave walls): wherever
   I do not find you, the silent
   mob that drifted mouthward – throngs
   loudly into time.

XIII River-noises, cool. A remnant
grief, merging
with the not yet nameable.
Barge wake, silt, and autumn. Head-
waters churn, a strand
of kelp
wheels over the rank
whey of foam – as one, nail-pierced
shard, twice, floats past you, salvaging
asylum
in eyes washed clean
of bliss.

xiv Mirrored by the tent-speech
    of our forty-dark, alodial-hued
    next year --
    the images,
    ground in the afterlight
    of eyes, the wandered
    images absolve you: (dunes
    that whirled free, – scree-words
    shuttled
    by the grate of sand, – the other
    glass-round hours, redoubling
    in remembrance). And in
    my hand – (as, after the night, – the night) –
    I hold what you have taken
    to give: this path
    of tallied cries, and grain
    after grain, the never-done-with
    desert, burning on your lips
    that jell in violence.

xv Frail dawn: the boundary
   of your darkened lamp: air
   without word: a rose-round, folding
   corolla of ash. From the smallest
   of your suns, you clench
   the scald: husk
   of relented light: the true seed
   in your fallow palm, deepening
   into dumbness. Beyond this hour, the eye
   will teach you. The eye will learn
   to long.

XVI Notched out
        on this crust of field – in the day
        that comes after us,
        where you saw the earth
        almost happen again: the echoing
        furrows have closed,
        and for this one-more-life, have ransomed you
        against the avid murmur
        of scythes. Count me along, then,
        with your words. Nothing,
        even on this day, will change.
        Shoulder
        to shoulder with dust, before
        the blade, and beyond
        the tall dry grass
        that veers with me, I am the air's
        stammered relic.

XVII   Evening, at half-mast
       through mulberry-glow and lichen: the banner
       of the unpronounceable
       future. The skull's
       rabble
       crept out from you – doubling
       across the threshold – and became
       your knell
       among the many: you
       never heard it
       again. Anti-stars
       above the city you expel
       from language, turning, at odds,
       even with you, repeal the arson-
       eye's quiet
       testimony.

xviii Rats wake in your sleep
       and mime the progress
       of want. My voice turns back
       to the hunger it gives birth to,
       coupling with stones
       that jut from red walls: the heart
       gnaws, but cannot know
       its plunder; the flayed tongue
       rasps. We lie
       in earth's deepest marrow, and listen
       to the breath of angels.
       Our bones have been drained.
       Wherever night has spoken,
       unborn sons prowl the void
       between stars.

xix The dead still die: and in them
    the living. All space,
    and the eyes, hunted
    by brittle tools, confined
    to their habits.
    To breathe is to accept
    this lack of air, the only breath,
    sought in the fissures
    of memory, in the lapse that sunders
    this language of feuds, without which earth
    would have granted a stronger omen
    to level the orchards
    of stone. Not even
    the silence pursues me.

xx Immune to the craving
    gray of fog, hate, uttered
    in the eaves, day-
    long, kept you near. We
    knew that sun
    had wormed through the shuttered panes
    in drunkenness
    only. We knew a deeper void
    was being
    built by the gulls who scavenged
    their own cries. We knew that they
    knew the landfall
    was mirage.
    And was waiting,
    from the first hour
    I had come to you. My skin,
    shuddering in the light.
    The light, shattering at my touch.

XXI No one's voice, alien
       to fall, and once
       gathered in the eye that bled
       such brightness. Your sinew
       does not mend, it is
       another rope, braided
       by ink, and aching through
       this raw hand – that hauls the images
       back to us: the clairvoyant
       corpse, singing
       from his gallows-mirror; a glance,
       heavier than stone, hurled
       down to April
       ice, ringing the bottom
       of your breath-well; an eye,
       and then
       one more. Till vulture
       is the word
       that gluts this offal, night
       will be your prey.

XXII Nomad –
    till nowhere, blooming
    in the prison of your mouth, becomes
    wherever you are: you
    read the fable
    that was written in the eyes
    of dice: (it was
    the meteor-word, scrawled by light
    between us, yet we, in the end,
    had no evidence, we
    could not produce
    the stone). The die-and-the-die
    now own your name. As if to say,
    wherever you are
    the desert is with you. As if,
    wherever you move, the desert
    is new,
    is moving with you.

White Nights

No one here,
and the body says: whatever is said
is not to be said. But no one
is a body as well, and what the body says
is heard by no one
but you.

Snowfall and night. The repetition
of a murder
among the trees. The pen
moves across the earth: it no longer knows
what will happen, and the hand that holds it
has disappeared.

Nevertheless, it writes.
It writes: in the beginning,
among the trees, a body came walking
from the night. It writes:
the body's whiteness
is the color of earth. It is earth,
and the earth writes: everything
is the color of silence.

I am no longer here. I have never said
what you say
I have said. And yet, the body is a place
where nothing dies. And each night,
from the silence of the trees, you know
that my voice
comes walking toward you.

Matrix and Dream

Inaudible things, chipped
nightly away:
breath, underground
through winter: well-words
down the quarried light
of lullaby rill
and chasm.

You pass.
Between fear and memory,
the agate
of your footfall turns
crimson
in the dust of childhood.

Thirst: and coma: and leaf –
from the gaps
of the no longer known: the unsigned message,
buried in my body.

The white linen
hanging on the line. The wormwood
crushed
in the field.

The smell of mint
from the ruin.

Interior

Grappled flesh
of the fully other and one.
And each thing here, as if it were the last thing
to be said: the sound of a word
married to death, and the life
that is this force in me
to disappear.

Shutters closed. The dust
of a former self, emptying the space
I do not fill. This light
that grows in the corner of the room,
where the whole of the room
has moved.

Night repeats. A voice that speaks to me
only of smallest things.
Not even things – but their names.
And where no names are –
of stones. The clatter of goats
climbing through the villages
of noon. A scarab
devoured in the sphere
of its own dung. And the violet swarm
of butterflies beyond.

In the impossibility of words,
in the unspoken word
that asphyxiates,
I find myself.

Pulse

This that recedes
will come near to us
on the other side of day.

Autumn: a single leaf
eaten by light: and the green
gaze of green upon us.
Where earth does not stop,
we, too, will become this light,
even as the light
dies
in the shape of a leaf.

Gaping eye
in the hunger of day.
Where we have not been
we will be. A tree
will take root in us
and rise in the light
of our mouths.

The day will stand before us.
The day will follow us
into the day.

Scribe

The name
never left his lips: he talked himself
into another body: he found his room again
in Babel.

It was written.
A flower
falls from his eye
and blooms in a stranger's mouth.
A swallow
rhymes with hunger
and cannot leave its egg.

He invents
the orphan in tatters,

he will hold
a small black flag
riddled with winter.

It is spring,
and below his window
he hears
a hundred white stones
turn to raging phlox.

Choral

Whinnied by flint,
in the dream-gait that cantered you across
the clover-swarmed
militant field:

this bit
of earth that inches up
to us again, shattered
by the shrill, fife-sharp tone
that jousts you open, million-fold,
in your utmost
heretic word.

Slowly,
you dip your finger into the wound
from which my voice
escapes.

Meridian

All summer long,
by the gradient rasp-light
of our dark, dune-begetting hands: your stones,
crumbling back to life
around you.

Behind my sheer, raven lid,
one early star,
flushed from a hell of briars,
rears you up, innocent,
towards morning, and peoples your shadow
with names.

Night-rhymed. Harrow-deep.
Near.

Lackawanna

Scree-rails, rust,
remembrance: the no longer bearable, again,
shunting across
your gun-metal earth. The eye
does not will
what enters it: it must always refuse
to refuse.

In the burgeoning frost
of equinox: you will have your name,
and nothing more. Dwarfed
to the reddening seed-space
in which every act
rebuts you, your hot, image-bright pore
again
will force its way

open.

Lies. Decrees. 1972.

Imagine:
the conscripting word
that camped in the squalor
of his fathom-moaned, unapproachable
heaven
goes on warring
in time.

Imagine:
even now
he does not repent of
his oath, even
now, he stammers back, unwitnessed, to his
resurrected throne.

Imagine:
the murdered ones,
cursed and radiant below him,
usher the knives
of their humbled, birth-marked silence, deep
into the alleyways
of his mouth.

Imagine:
I speak this to you,
from the evening of the first day,
undyingly,
along the short, human fuse
of resistance.

Ecliptic. Les Halles.

You were my absence.
Wherever I breathed, you found me
lying in the word
that spoke its way back
to this place.

Silence
was
in the prowled shambles
and marrow
of a cunning, harlot haste – a hunger
that became
a bed for me,

as though the random
Ezekiel-wrath
I discovered, the 'Live,' and the
'yes, he said to us,
when we were in our blood,
Live,' had merely been your way
of coming near –

as though somewhere,
visible, an arctic stone, as pale
as semen, had been
dripping, fire-phrase by fire-phrase,
from your lips.

Dictum: After Great Distances

Oleander and rose. The rubble
of earth's other air – where the hummingbird
flies in the shadow
of the hawk. And through each wall, the opening
earth of August,
like a stone that cracks
this wall of sun.

Mountains. And then the lights
of the town
beyond the mountain. The town that lies
on the other side
of light.

We dream
that we do not dream. We wake
in the hours of sleep
and sleep through the silence
that stands over us. Summer
keeps its promise
by breaking it.

Fore-shadows

I breathe you.
I becalm you out of me.
I numb you in the reach
of brethren light.
I suckle you
to the dregs of disaster.

The sky pins a vagrant star
on my chest. I see the wind
as witness, the towering night
that lapsed
in a maze of oaks,
the distance.

I haunt you
to the brink of sorrow.
I milk you of strength.
I defy you,
I deify you
to nothing and
to no one,

I become
your necessary and most violent
heir.

Ireland

Turf-spent, moor-abandoned you,
you, the more naked one, bathed in the dark
of the greenly overrun
deep-glen, of the gray bed
my ghost
pilfered from the mouths
of stones – bestow on me the silence
to shoulder the wings of rooks, allow me
to pass through here again
and breathe the rankly dealt-with air
that still traffics in your shame,
give me the right to destroy you
on the tongue that impales
our harvest, the merciless
acres of cold.

Prism

Earth-time, the stones
tick
in hollows of dust, the arable air
wanders far from home, barbed
wire and road
are erased. Spat
out by the burning
fever in our lungs, the Ur-seed
blooms from crystal, our vermilion breath
refracts us
into many. We will not
ever know ourselves
again. Like the light
that moves between the bars
of light
we sometimes called death,
we, too, will have flowered,
even with such
unquenchable flames
as these.

Wall Writing

Nothing less than nothing.

In the night that comes
from nothing,
for no one in the night
that does not come.

And what stands at the edge of whiteness,
invisible
in the eye of the one who speaks.

Or a word.

Come from nowhere
in the night
of the one who does not come.

Or the whiteness of a word,
scratched
into the wall.

Covenant

Throng of eyes,
myriad, at sunken retina depth: the image
of the great, imageless one,
moored within.

Mantis-lunged, we,
the hirelings, alive in juniper and rubble,
broke the flat bread
that went with us, we
were steps, wandered
into blindness, we knew by then
how to breathe ourselves along
to nothing.

Something lost
became
something to be found.
A name,
followed through the dust
of all that veering, did not ever
divulge its sound. The mountain
was the spoor
by which an animal pain
hunted itself home.

All night
I read the braille wounds
on the inner wall
of your cry, and at the brink
of the thick, millenial morning, climbed up
into you again, where all

my bones began
beating and
beating the heart-drum
to shreds.

Hieroglyph

The language of walls.
Or one last word –
cut
from the visible.

May Day. The metamorphosis
of Solomon's-seal
into stone. The just
doom of the uttered
road, unraveled in the swirl
of pollen-memory
and seed. Do not
emerge, Eden. Stay
in the mouths of the lost
who dream you.

Upon thunder and thorn: the furtive air
arms
the lightning-gorse and silence
of each fallow sky
below. Blood Hebrew. Or what
translates
my body's turning back
to an image of earth.

This knife
I hold against your throat.

White

For one who drowned:
this page, as if
thrown out to sea
in a bottle.

So that
even as the sky embarks
into the seeing of earth, an echo
of the earth
might sail toward him,
filled with a memory of rain,
and the sound of the rain
falling on the water.

So that
he will have learned,
in spite of the wave
now sinking from the crest
of mountains, that forty days
and forty nights
have brought no dove
back to us.

Pastoral

In the hinterland of moss and waiting,
so little like the word
that was a waiting as well,
all has been other
than it is, the moss
still waits for you, the word
is a lantern
you carry to the depths
of green, for even the roots
have carried light, and even now
your voice
still travels through the roots, so that
wherever an axe may fall
you, too, shall know that you live.

Incendiary

Flint hours. The dumb sprawl
of stones around us, heart
against heart, we, in the straw
hulk
that festers through the damp
lapse of night.

Nothing left. The cold eye
opens on cold,
as an image of fire
eats
through the word
that struggles in your mouth. The world
is
whatever you leave to it, is only
you
in the world my body
enters: this place
where all is lacking.

Song of Degrees

In the vacant lots
of solstice. In the light
you wagered for the rubble
of awe. Sand heaps:
retched into prayer – the distance
bought
in your name.

You. And then
you again. A footstep
gives ground: what is more
is not more: nothing
has ever been
enough. Tents,
pitched and struck: a ladder
propped
on a pillow of stone: the sheer
aureole rungs
of fire. You,
and then we. The earth
does not ask
for anyone.

So
be it. So much
the better – so many
words,
raked and murmured along
by your bedouin knees, will not
conjure you home. Even
if you crawled from the skin

of your brother,
you would not go beyond
what you breathe: no
angel can cure you
of your name.

Minima. Memory
and mirage. In each place
you stop for air,
we will build a city
around you. Through the star-
mortared wall
that rises in our night, your soul
will not pass
again.

Fire Speech

You veer out. You crumble in.
You stand.

Cradled
by the hour-gong
that beat through the holly
twelve times
more silent than you, something, let
loose by someone,
rescues your name from coal.

You stand
there again, breathing
in the phantom sun
between ice and reverie.

I have come so far for you,
the voice
that echoes back to me
is no longer my own.

Lapsarian

This bit-open earth.
Arbor: in the neigh of branches.
The shallow night, merging
with noon.

I speak to you
of the word that mires in the smell
of here-after.
I speak to you of the fruit
I shoveled up
from below.
I speak to you of speech.

Humus colors. Buried in the rift
till human. The day's
prismatic blessing – divisible
by breath. Starling paths,
snake furrows, seeds. The quick
skewers of flame. What burns
is banished.
Is taken with you.
Is yours.

A man
walks out from the voice
that became me.
He has vanished.
He has eaten

the ripening word
that killed you and
killed you.

He has found himself,
standing in the place
where the eye most terribly holds
its ground.

Late Summer

Borealis flood, and all of night, unleashed
at the eye's diluvian hour. Our bone-
broken will, countering the flow
of stones within our blood: vertigo
from the helium heights
of language.

Tomorrow: a mountain road
lined with gorse. Sunlight
in the fissures of rock. Lessness.
As if we could hold a single breath
to the limit of breath.

There is no promised land.

Heraclitian

All earth, accountable
to greenness, the air's ballast
coal, and the winter
that ignites
the fire of earth, as all air moves
unbrokenly
into the green
moment of ourselves. We know that we are
spoken for. And we know that earth
will never yield
a word
small enough to hold us. For the just word
is only of air, and in the green
ember
of our nether sameness, it brings no fear
but that of life. We therefore
will be named
by all that we are not. And whoever
sees himself
in what is not yet
spoken,
will know what it is
to fear
earth
to the just
measure of himself.

Braille

Legibility of earth. Bone's
clear pelt,
and the swerve of plume-and-weal clouds
in victim air – no longer
to be read.

'When you stop on this road,
the road, from that moment on,
will vanish.'

And you knew, then,
that there were two of us: you knew
that from all this flesh of air, I
had found the place
where one word
was growing wild.

Nine months darker, my mouth bores through
the bright ways
that cross with yours. Nine lives
deeper, the cry is still
the same.

Salvage

Reunion of ash men
and ash women. Sky's wan hub
grown full till anther-round
on the peat slope from which
I saw them. May-green: what was said,
audible in the eye. The words,
mingled with snow, did not
indict the mouth. I drank
the wine they begrudged me. I stood, perhaps,
beside where you
might have been. I dragged
everything
home to the other world.

Autobiography of the Eye

Invisible things, rooted in cold,
and growing toward this light
that vanishes
into each thing
it illumines. Nothing ends. The hour
returns to the beginning
of the hour in which we breathed: as if
there were nothing. As if I could see
nothing
that is not what it is.

At the limit of summer
and its warmth: blue sky, purple hill.
The distance that survives.
A house, built of air, and the flux
of the air in the air.

Like these stones
that crumble back into earth.
Like the sound of my voice
in your mouth.

All Souls

Anonymity and floe: November
by its only name, death-
danced
through the broken speech
of hoe and furrow
down
from the eaves of overwhelming – these
hammer-worshipped
spew-things
cast
into the zones of blood.

A transfusion of darkness,
the generate peace, encroaching
on slaughter.

Life equal to life.

Disappearances

1 Out of solitude, he begins again –

as if it were the last time
that he would breathe,

and therefore it is now

that he breathes for the first time
beyond the grasp
of the singular.

He is alive, and therefore he is nothing
but what drowns in the fathomless hole
of his eye,

and what he sees
is all that he is not: a city

of the undeciphered
event,

and therefore a language of stones,
since he knows that for the whole of life
a stone
will give way to another stone

to make a wall

and that all these stones
will form the monstrous sum

of particulars.

2 It is a wall. And the wall is death.

Illegible
scrawl of discontent, in the image

and after-image of life –

and the many who are here
though never born,
and those who would speak

to give birth to themselves.

He will learn the speech of this place.
And he will learn to hold his tongue.

For this is his nostalgia: a man.

3 To hear the silence
that follows the word of oneself. Murmur

of the least stone

shaped in the image
of earth, and those who would speak
to be nothing

but the voice that speaks them
to the air.

And he will tell
of each thing he sees in this space,
and he will tell it to the very wall
that grows before him:

and for this, too, there will be a voice,
although it will not be his.

Even though he speaks.

And because he speaks.

4 There are the many – and they are here:

and for each stone he counts among them
he excludes himself,

as if he, too, might begin to breathe
for the first time

in the space that separates him
from himself.

For the wall is a word. And there is no word
he does not count
as a stone in the wall.

Therefore, he begins again,
and at each moment he begins to breathe

he feels there has never been another
time – as if for the time that he lived
he might find himself

in each thing he is not.

What he breathes, therefore,
is time, and he knows now
that if he lives

it is only in what lives

and will continue to live
without him.

5   In the face of the wall –

    he divines the monstrous
    sum of particulars.

    It is nothing.
    And it is all that he is.
    And if he would be nothing, then let him begin
    where he finds himself, and like any other man
    learn the speech of this place.

    For he, too, lives in the silence
    that comes before the word
    of himself.

6　And of each thing he has seen
　　he will speak –

　　the blinding
　　enumeration of stones,
　　even to the moment of death –

　　as if for no other reason
　　than that he speaks.

　　Therefore, he says I,
　　and counts himself
　　in all that he excludes,

　　which is nothing,

　　and because he is nothing
　　he can speak, which is to say
　　there is no escape

　　from the word that is born
　　in the eye. And whether or not
　　he would say it,

　　there is no escape.

7   He is alone. And from the moment he begins to
    breathe,

    he is nowhere. Plural death, born

    in the jaws of the singular,

    and the word that would build a wall
    from the innermost stone
    of life.

    For each thing that he speaks of
    he is not –

    and in spite of himself
    he says I, as if he, too, would begin
    to live in all the others

    who are not. For the city is monstrous,
    and its mouth suffers
    no issue

    that does not devour the word
    of oneself.

    Therefore, there are the many,
    and all these many lives
    shaped into the stones
    of a wall,

and he who would begin to breathe
will learn there is nowhere to go
but here.

Therefore, he begins again,

as if it were the last time
he would breathe.

For there is no more time. And it is the end of time

that begins.

Northern Lights

These are the words
that do not survive the world. And to speak them
is to vanish

into the world. Unapproachable
light
that heaves above the earth, kindling
the brief miracle

of the open eye –

and the day that will spread
like a fire of leaves
through the first chill wind
of October

consuming the world

in the plain speech
of desire.

Reminiscence of Home

True north. Vincent's north.
The glimpsed

unland of light. And through each fissure
of earth, the indigo
fields that burn
in a seething wind of stars.

What is locked
in the eye that possessed you
still serves
as an image of home: the barricade
of an empty chair, and the father, absent,
still blooming in his urn
of honesty.

You will close your eyes.
In the eye of the crow who flies before you,
you will watch yourself
leave yourself behind.

Effigies

Eucalyptus roads: a remnant of the pale sky
shuddering in my throat. Through the ballast
drone of summer

the weeds that silence
even your step.

*

The myriad haunts of light.
And each lost thing – a memory

of what has never been. The hills. The impossible
hills

lost in the brilliance of memory

*

As if it were all

still to be born. Deathless in the eye,
where the eye now opens on the noise

of heat: a wasp, a thistle swaying on the prongs

of barbed wire.

*

Snowfall. And in the nethermost
lode of whiteness – a memory
that adds your steps
to the lost.

*

Endlessly
I would have walked with you.

*

Alba. The immense, alluvial light. The carillon
of clouds at dawn. And the boats
moored in the jetty fog

are invisible. And if they are there

they are invisible.

Gnomon

September sun, illusionless. The purple
field awash
in the hours of the first breath. You will not
submit to this light, or close your eyes
to the vigilant
crumbling of light in your eyes.

Firmament of fact. And you,
like everything else
that moves. Parsed seed
and thimble of air. Fissured
cloud and worm: the open-
ended sentence that engulfs you
at the moment I begin
to be silent.

Perhaps, then, a world
that secretes its harvest
in the lungs, a means
of survival by breath
alone. And if nothing,
then let nothing be
the shadow
that walks inside your shadow, the body
that will cast
the first stone, so that even as you walk
away from yourself, you might feel it
hunger toward you, hourly,
across the enormous
vineyards of the living.

Fragment from Cold

Because we go blind
in the day that goes out with us,
and because we have seen our breath
cloud
the mirror of air,
the eye of the air will open
on nothing but the word
we renounce: winter
will have been a place
of ripeness.

We who become the dead
of another life than ours.

Aubade

Not even the sky.
But a memory of sky,
and the blue of the earth
in your lungs.

Earth
less earth: to watch
how the sky will enclose you, grow vast
with the words
you leave unsaid – and nothing
will be lost.

I am your distress, the seam
in the wall
that opens to the wind
and its stammering, storm
in the plural – this other name
you give your world: exile
in the rooms of home.

Dawn folds, fathers
witness,
the aspen and the ash
that fall. I come back to you
through this fire, a remnant
of the season to come,
and will be to you
as dust, as air,
as nothing

that will not haunt you.
In the place before breath
we feel our shadows cross.

Transfusion

Oven's glow. Or vast
hemoglobin
leap –

:the blasphemy
of their death-devoted word, lying
in the self-same blood
your open heart
still squanders.

Pulse –
and then what – (then
what?) – erupts in the skull
of the ghetto sphinx – that plumbs
the filth
and fever of the ones
who gave up. (Like you,
they still hover, still
hunger, immured in the bread
of no one's flesh, still make themselves
felt):

as if, in the distance between
sundown and sunrise,
a hand
had gathered up your soul
and worked it with the stones
into the leaven
of earth.

Siberian

Shadow, carted off by wolves,
and quartered, half a life beyond
each barb of the wire, now I see you,
magnetic
polar felon, now I begin
to speak to you
of the wild boar
of southern woods, of scrub
oak and thicket spruce, of thyme-reek
and lavender, even
down to lava, spewn, through each
chink in the wall, so that you, counter-voice, lost
in the cold
of farthest murder, might come
floating back
on your barge of ice, bearing
the untellable
cargo of forgiveness.

Clandestine

Remember with me today – the word
and counter-word
of witness: the tactile dawn, emerging
from my clenched hand: sun's
ciliary grasp: the stretch of darkness
I wrote
on the table of sleep.

Now
is the time to come.
All you have come
to take from me, take
away from me now. Do not
forget
to forget. Fill
your pockets with earth,
and seal up the mouth
of my cave.

It was there
I dreamed my life
into a dream
of fire.

Quarry

No more than the song of it. As if
the singing alone
had led us back to this place.

We have been here, and we have never been here.
We have been on the way to where we began,
and we have been lost.

There are no boundaries
in the light. And the earth
leaves no word for us
to sing. For the crumbling of the earth
underfoot

is a music in itself, and to walk among these stones
is to hear nothing
but ourselves.

I sing, therefore, of nothing,

as if it were the place
I do not return to –

and if I should return, then count out my life
in these stones: forget
I was ever here. The world
that walks inside me

is a world beyond reach.

White Spaces

Something happens, and from the moment it begins to happen, nothing can ever be the same again.

Something happens. Or else, something does not happen. A body moves. Or else, it does not move. And if it moves, something begins to happen. And even if it does not move, something begins to happen.

It comes from my voice. But that does not mean these words will ever be what happens. It comes and goes. If I happen to be speaking at this moment, it is only because I hope to find a way of going along, of running parallel to everything else that is going along, and so begin to find a way of filling the silence without breaking it.

I ask whoever is listening to this voice to forget the words it is speaking. It is important that no one listen too carefully. I want these words to vanish, so to speak, into the silence they came from, and for nothing to remain but a memory of their presence, a token of the fact that they were once here and are here no longer and that during their brief life they seemed not so much to be saying any particular thing as to be the thing that was happening at the same time a certain body was moving in a certain space, that they moved along with everything else that moved.

Something begins, and already it is no longer the beginning, but something else, propelling us into the heart of the thing that is happening. If we were suddenly to stop and ask ourselves, 'Where are we going?', or 'Where are we now?', we would be lost, for at each moment we are no longer where we were, but have left ourselves behind, irrevocably, in a past that has no memory, a past endlessly obliterated by a motion that carries us into the present.

It will not do, then, to ask questions. For this is a landscape of random impulse, of knowledge for its own sake – which is to say, a knowledge that exists, that comes into being beyond any possibility of putting it into words. And if just this once we were to abandon ourselves to the supreme indifference of simply being wherever we happen to be, then perhaps we would not be deluding ourselves into thinking that we, too, had at last become a part of it all.

To think of motion not merely as a function of the body but as an extension of the mind. In the same way, to think of speech not as an extension of the mind but as a function of the body. Sounds emerge from the voice to enter the air and surround and bounce off and enter the body that occupies that air, and though they cannot be seen, these sounds are no less a gesture than a hand is when outstretched in the air towards another hand, and in this gesture can be read the entire alphabet of desire, the body's need to be taken beyond itself, even as it dwells in the sphere of its own motion.

On the surface, this motion seems to be random. But such randomness does not, in itself, preclude a meaning. Or if meaning is not quite the word for it, then say the drift, or a consistent sense of what is happening, even as it changes, moment by moment. To describe it in all its details is probably not impossible. But so many words would be needed, so many streams of syllables, sentences, and subordinate clauses, that the words would always lag behind what was happening, and long after all motion had stopped and each of its witnesses had dispersed, the voice describing that motion would still be speaking, alone, heard by no one, deep into the silence and darkness of these four walls. And yet something is happening, and in spite of myself I want to be present inside the space of this moment, of these moments, and to say something, even though it will be forgotten, that will form a part of this journey for the length of the time it endures.

In the realm of the naked eye nothing happens that does not have its beginning and its end. And yet nowhere can we find the place or the moment at which we can say, beyond a shadow of a doubt, that this is where it begins, or this is where it ends. For some of us, it has begun before the beginning, and for others of us it will go on happening after the end. Where to find it? Don't look. Either it is here or it is not here. And whoever tries to find refuge in any one place, in any one moment, will never be where he thinks he is. In other words, say your goodbyes. It is never too late. It is always too late.

To say the simplest thing possible. To go no farther than whatever it is I happen to find before me. To begin with this landscape, for example. Or even to note the things that are most near, as if in the tiny world before my eyes I might find an image of the life that exists beyond me, as if in a way I do not fully understand each thing in my life were connected to every other thing, which in turn connected me to the world at large, the endless world that looms up in the mind, as lethal and unknowable as desire itself.

To put it another way. It is sometimes necessary not to name the thing we are talking about. The invisible God of the Hebrews, for example, had an unpronounceable name, and each of the ninety-nine names tradition ascribes to this God was in fact nothing more than a way of acknowledging that-which-cannot-be-spoken, that-which-cannot-be-seen, and that-which-cannot-be-understood. But even on a less exalted plane, in the realm of the visible itself, we often hold back from divulging the thing we are talking about. Consider the word 'it'. 'It' is raining, we say, or how is 'it' going? We feel we know what we are saying, and what we mean to say is that it, the word 'it', stands for something that need not be said, or something that cannot be said. But if the thing we say is something that eludes us, something we do not understand, how can we persist in saying that we understand what we are saying? And yet it goes without saying that we do. The 'it', for example, in the preceding sentence, 'it goes without saying', is in fact nothing less than whatever it is that propels us into the act of speech itself. And if it, the word 'it', is what continually recurs in any effort to define it, then it must be accepted as the given, the precondition of the saying of it. It has been said, for example, that words falsify the thing they attempt to say, but even to say 'they falsify' is to admit that 'they falsify' is true, thus betraying an implicit faith in the power of words to say what they mean to say. And yet, when we speak, we often do not mean to say anything, as in the present case, in which I find these words falling from my mouth and vanishing into the silence they came from. In other words, it says itself, and our mouths are merely the instruments of the saying of it. How does it happen? But never do we ask what 'it' happens to be. We know, even if we cannot put it into words. And the feeling that remains within us, the discretion of a knowledge so fully in tune with the world, has no need of whatever it is that might fall from our mouths. Our hearts know what is in them, even if our mouths remain silent. And the world will know what it is, even when nothing remains in our hearts.

A man sets out on a journey to a place he has never been before. Another man comes back. A man comes to a place that has no name, that has no landmarks to tell him where he is. Another man decides to come back. A man writes letters from nowhere, from the white space that has opened up in his mind. The letters are never received. The letters are never sent. Another man sets out on a journey in search of the first man. This second man becomes more and more like the first man, until he, too, is swallowed up by the whiteness. A third man sets out on a journey with no hope of ever getting anywhere. He wanders. He continues to wander. For as long as he remains in the realm of the naked eye, he continues to wander.

I remain in the room in which I am writing this. I put one foot in front of the other. I put one word in front of the other, and for each step I take I add another word, as if for each word to be spoken there were another space to be crossed, a distance to be filled by my body as it moves through this space. It is a journey through space, even if I get nowhere, even if I end up in the same place I started. It is a journey through space, as if into many cities and out of them, as if across deserts, as if to the edge of some imaginary ocean, where each thought drowns in the relentless waves of the real.

I put one foot in front of the other, and then I put the other foot in front of the first, which has now become the other and which will again become the first. I walk within these four walls, and for as long as I am here I can go anywhere I like. I can go from one end of the room to the other and touch any of the four walls, or even all the walls, one after the other, exactly as I like. If the spirit moves me, I can stand in the center of the room. If the spirit moves me in another direction, I can stand in any one of the four corners. Sometimes I touch one of those four corners and in this way bring myself into contact with two walls at the same time. Now and then I let my eyes roam up to the ceiling, and when I am particularly exhausted by my efforts there is always the floor to welcome my body. The light, streaming through the windows, never casts the same shadow twice, and at any given moment I feel myself on the brink of discovering some terrible, unimagined truth. These are moments of great happiness for me.

Somewhere, as if unseen, and yet closer to us than we realize (down the street, for example, or in the next neighborhood), someone is being born. Somewhere else, a car is speeding along an empty highway in the middle of the night. In that same night, a man is hammering a nail into a board. We know nothing about any of this. A seed stirs invisibly in the earth, and we know nothing about it. Flowers wilt, buildings go up, children cry. And yet, for all that, we know nothing.

It happens, and as it continues to happen, we forget where we were when we began. Later, when we have traveled from this moment as far as we have traveled from the beginning, we will forget where we are now. Eventually, we will all go home, and if there are those among us who do not have a home, it is certain, nevertheless, that they will leave this place to go wherever it is they must. If nothing else, life has taught us all this one thing: whoever is here now will not be here later.

I dedicate these words to the things in life I do not understand, to each thing passing away before my eyes. I dedicate these words to the impossibility of finding a word equal to the silence inside me.

In the beginning, I wanted to speak of arms and legs, of jumping up and down, of bodies tumbling and spinning, of enormous journeys through space, of cities, of deserts, of mountain ranges stretching farther than the eye can see. Little by little, however, as these words began to impose themselves on me, the things I wanted to do seemed finally to be of no importance. Reluctantly, I abandoned all my witty stories, all my adventures of far-away places, and began, slowly and painfully, to empty my mind. Now emptiness is all that remains: a space, no matter how small, in which whatever is happening can be allowed to happen.

And no matter how small, each and every possibility remains. Even a motion reduced to an apparent absence of motion. A motion, for example, as minimal as breathing itself, the motion the body makes when inhaling and exhaling air. In a book I once read by Peter Freuchen, the famous Arctic explorer describes being trapped by a blizzard in northern Greenland. Alone, his supplies dwindling, he decided to build an igloo and wait out the storm. Many days passed. Afraid, above all, that he would be attacked by wolves – for he heard them prowling hungrily on the roof of his igloo – he would periodically step outside and sing at the top of his lungs in order to frighten them away. But the wind was blowing fiercely, and no matter how hard he sang, the only thing he could hear was the wind. If this was a serious problem, however, the problem of the igloo itself was much greater. For Freuchen began to notice that the walls of his little shelter were gradually closing in on him. Because of the particular weather conditions outside, his breath was literally freezing to the walls, and with each breath the walls became that much thicker, the igloo became that much smaller, until eventually there was almost no room left for his body. It is surely a frightening thing, to imagine breathing yourself into a coffin of ice, and to my mind considerably more compelling than, say, *The Pit and the Pendulum* by Poe. For in this case it is the man himself who is the agent of his own destruction, and further, the instrument of that destruction is the very thing he needs to keep himself alive. For surely a man cannot live if he does not breathe. But at the same time, he will not live if he does breathe. Curiously, I do not remember how Freuchen managed to escape his predicament. But needless to say, he did escape. The title of the book, if I recall, is *Arctic Adventure*. It has been out of print for many years.

Nothing happens. And still, it is not nothing. To invoke things that have never happened is noble, but how much sweeter to remain in the realm of the naked eye.

It comes down to this: that everything should count, that everything should be a part of it, even the things I do not or cannot understand. The desire, for example, to destroy every-thing I have written so far. Not from any revulsion at the inadequacy of these words (although that remains a distinct possibility), but rather from the need to remind myself, at each moment, that things do not have to happen this way, that there is always another way, neither better nor worse, in which things might take shape. I realize in the end that I am probably powerless to affect the outcome of even the least thing that happens, but nevertheless, and in spite of myself, as if in an act of blind faith, I want to assume full responsibility. And therefore this desire, this overwhelming need, to take these papers and scatter them across the room. Or else, to go on. Or else, to begin again. Or else, to go on, as if each moment were the beginning, as if each word were the beginning of another silence, another word more silent than the last.

A few scraps of paper. A last cigarette before turning in. The snow falling endlessly in the winter night. To remain in the realm of the naked eye, as happy as I am at this moment. And if this is too much to ask, then to be granted the memory of it, a way of returning to it in the darkness of the night that will surely engulf me again. Never to be anywhere but here. And the immense journey through space that continues. Everywhere, as if each place were here. And the snow falling endlessly in the winter night.

Credo

The infinite

tiny things. For once merely to breathe
in the light of the infinite

tiny things
that surround us. Or nothing
can escape

the lure of this darkness, the eye
will discover that we are
only what has made us less
than we are. To say nothing. To say:
our very lives

depend on it.

Obituary in the Present Tense

It is all one to him –
where he begins

and where he ends. Egg white, the white
of his eye: he says
bird milk, sperm

sliding from the word
of himself. For the eye
is evanescent,
clings only to what is, no more here

or less there, but everywhere, every

thing. He memorizes
none of it. Nor does he write

anything down. He abstains
from the heart

of living things. He waits.

And if he begins, he will end,
as if his eye had opened in the mouth

of a bird, as if he had never begun

to be anywhere. He speaks
from distances
no less far than these.

Narrative

Because what happens will never happen,
and because what has happened
endlessly happens again,

we are as we were, everything
has changed in us, if we speak
of the world
it is only to leave the world

unsaid. Early winter: the yellow apples still
unfallen
in a naked tree, the tracks
of invisible deer

in the first snow, and then the snow
that does not stop. We repent
of nothing. As if we could stand
in this light. As if we could stand in the silence
of this single moment

of light.

S. A. 1911–1979

From loss. And from such loss
that marauds the mind – even to the loss

of mind. To begin with this thought: without rhyme

or reason. And then simply to wait. As if the first
    word
comes only after the last, after a life
of waiting for the word

that was lost. To say no more
than the truth of it: men die, the world fails, the
    words

have no meaning. And therefore to ask
only for words.

Stone wall. Stone heart. Flesh and blood.

As much as all this.
More.

Search for a Definition

(On Seeing a Painting by Bradley Walker Tomlin)

Always the smallest act

possible
in this time of acts

larger than life, a gesture
toward the thing that passes

almost unseen. A small wind

disturbing a bonfire, for example,
which I found the other day
by accident

on a museum wall. Almost nothing
is there: a few wisps
of white

thrown idly against the pure black
background, no more
than a small gesture
trying to be nothing

more than itself. And yet
it is not here
and to my eyes will never become
a question
of trying to simplify

the world, but a way of looking for a place
to enter the world, a way of being
present
among the things
that do not want us – but which we need
to the same measure that we need
ourselves. Only a moment before
the beautiful

woman
who stood before me
had been saying how much she wanted
a child
and how time was beginning
to run out on her. We said
we must each write a poem
using the words 'a small
wind

disturbing a bonfire'. Since that time
nothing

has meant more than the small
act
present in these words, the act
of trying to speak

words

that mean almost nothing. To the very end
I want to be equal
to whatever it is
my eye will bring me, as if
I might finally see myself

let go
in the nearly invisible
things

that carry us along with ourselves and all
the unborn children

into the world.

Between the Lines

Stone-pillowed, the ways
of remoteness. And written in your palm,
the road.

Home, then, is not home
but the distance between
blessed
and unblessed. And whoever puts himself
into the skin
of his brother, will know
what sorrow is
to the seventh year
beyond the seventh year
of the seventh year.

And divide his children in half.

And wrestle in darkness
with an angel.

In Memory of Myself

Simply to have stopped.

As if I could begin
where my voice has stopped, myself
the sound of a word

I cannot speak.

So much silence
to be brought to life
in this pensive flesh, the beating
drum of words
within, so many words

lost in the wide world
within me, and thereby to have known
that in spite of myself

I am here.

As if this were the world.

Bedrock

Dawn as an image
of dawn, and the very sky collapsing
into itself. Irreducible

image
of pure water, the pores of earth
exuding light: such yield

as only light will bring, and the very stones
undead

in the image of themselves.

The consolation of color.

Facing the Music

Blue. And within that blue a feeling
of green, the gray blocks of clouds
buttressed against air, as if
in the idea of rain
the eye
could master the speech
of any given moment

on earth. Call it the sky. And so
to describe
whatever it is
we see, as if it were nothing
but the idea
of something we had lost
within. For we can begin
to remember

the hard earth, the flint
reflecting stars, the undulating
oaks set loose
by the heaving of air, and so down
to the least seed, revealing what grows
above us, as if
because of this blue there could be
this green

that spreads, myriad
and miraculous
in this, the most silent
moment of summer. Seeds
speak of this juncture, define

where the air and the earth erupt
in this profusion of chance, the random
forces of our own lack
of knowing what it is
we see, and merely to speak of it
is to see
how words fail us, how nothing comes right
in the saying of it, not even these words
I am moved to speak
in the name of this blue
and green
that vanish into the air
of summer.

                    Impossible
to hear it anymore. The tongue
is forever taking us away
from where we are, and nowhere
can we be at rest
in the things we are given
to see, for each word
is an elsewhere, a thing that moves
more quickly than the eye, even
as this sparrow moves, veering
into the air
in which it has no home. I believe, then,
in nothing

these words might give you, and still
I can feel them
speaking through me, as if
this alone
is what I desire, this blue
and this green, and to say
how this blue
has become for me the essence
of this green, and more than the pure

seeing of it, I want you to feel
this word
that has lived inside me
all day long, this
desire for nothing

but the day itself, and how it has grown
inside my eyes, stronger
than the word it is made of, as if
there could never be another word

that would hold me
without breaking.